Victoria Moffat

# ✚ First Aid Manual

## 7th Edition

## Preface

This fully illustrated manual has been written to provide concise and relevant guidance to employers and employees wishing to learn current first aid at work practices. The manual incorporates the principles of first aid required to pass a statutory first aid at work course, and should be used in conjunction with the practical training provided by an authorised training organisation.

This manual also contains a self-test quiz at the end of each section with full answers at the end, which can be used as an aide memoire by qualified first-aiders, or by students revising for their first aid exams.

## Disclaimer

The contents of this manual are to be used for guidance only and do not constitute formal first aid or medical training.

The advice given is the publisher's interpretation of current first aid at work practice and the publisher cannot accept liability for any errors or omissions.

## Acknowledgments

The publishers would like to thank the following professionals for their help and assistance in compiling this manual.

Mr C. Lamb MBChB, MRCGR, MFOM
Mr D.K. Evans FRCS
Mr D. Londesborough LLB(Hons)
Mrs V. Bertram BSC(Hons), RGN, OHNC
Mr C.J Cahill FRCS(Ed), FFAEM
Mr P. Coster IHCD
Ms Alex Forsyth BA(Hons) in Nursing
Mr John Howell IHCD Paramedic
Mr Justin Connelly IHCD Paramedic

## Edition

© Copyright 2016 Safety First Aid Group 7th Edition

# Contents

## 01 First Aider Responsibilities

## 02 First Aid Principles

## 03 Assessing A Casualty

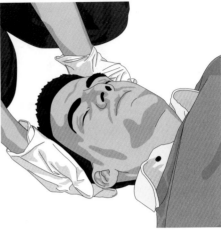

## 04 The Unresponsive Casualty

# 05 Respiratory Problems

# 06 Managing External & Internal Bleeding

# 07 Managing Bone Joint & Soft Tissue Injuries

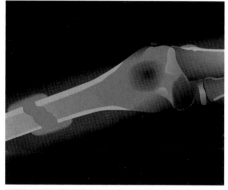

# 08 Burns

# 09 Poisoning

# 10 Other Injuries

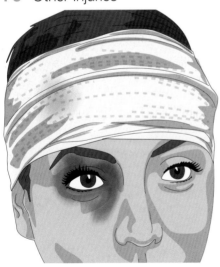

# 11 Conditions

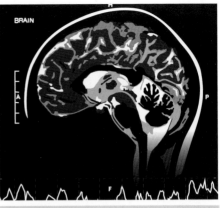

# 12 Sports First Aid

# 01 First Aider Responsibilities

This section looks at the administrative duties of a first aider. These include the maintenance of the first aid supplies and the importance of completing proper records. It also discusses appropriate ways of moving a casualty.

## Content

## Completing & Maintaining Records

What records do I have to keep?

All accidents at work should be reported in an appropriate DPA compliant accident book. Individual records should be removed and stored in a secure cabinet. The Health and Safety Executive (HSE) can inspect this book if they wish.

Some workplaces also have their own procedure following an accident such as completing a specific form or informing the Safety Officer or Occupational Health Department. You should familiarise yourself with your workplace policy for first aiders.

Under The Reporting of Injuries Diseases and Dangerous Occurrences Regulations (RIDDOR) 2013 certain first aid situations need reporting to the HSE either immediately or within 10 days dependent upon the type of incident. You should be aware of who your reporting officer is and the procedure for contacting them when incidents occur.

**All records should be legible and detail:**

+ The date, time and place of the accident.

+ The person or person's involved and contact details.

+ A summary of what happened.

+ Details of any witnesses.

+ Information about the apparent injury.

+ First aid treatment given and by whom.

+ Whether the person returned to work, was sent to hospital, to their doctor or home.

+ Any other information such as what happened to the hazard, or to whom the incident was reported.

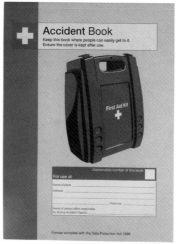

## British Standard Compliant First Aid Kits

### Complying with BS 8599-1, Workplace First Aid Kits

In recognising the need to ensure that current workplace first aid provision is adequate and appropriate The British Healthcare Trade Association has been working with the British Standards Institute (BSI), to create a new British Standard for first aid kits in the workplace.

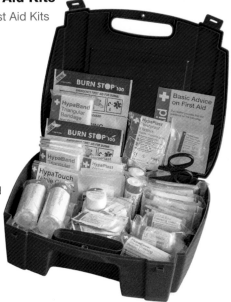

The contents of these new kits take into account more modern and functional products encompassing a wider range of common workplace risks and are therefore more comprehensive than the previous HSE compliant kits. BS 8599-1 is the standard that sets the new minimum level that workplace first aid kits should conform to.

The new standard, like the previous Health & Safety Executive (HSE) L74 Approved Code of Practice, gives recommendations on the amount and size of the first aid kits necessary for the different workplace environments based on the category of risk and number of employees in the workplace.

Should the risk or numbers of employee deem it necessary, the minimum contents as set out in the standard can be supplemented by additional items appropriate to the hazards identified by the risk assessment. This may result for example in increasing the number of burn dressings where a significant risk of a burn injury is likely.

### What size kit do I need?

The size of the kit required is dependent on a combination of the level of risk and the number of employees in the workplace. The table below provides guidance for employers but does not replace the requirement to carry out a risk assessment.

This table is for guidance only and each workplace needs to evaluate its own level of risk.

| Category Of Hazard | Number of Employees | Number & Size of First Aid Kit |
|---|---|---|
| **Low Hazard** – e.g. shops, offices, libraries | Less than 25 | 1 Small Kit |
| | 25-100 | 1 Medium Kit |
| | More than 100 | 1 Large Kit per 100 employees |
| **High Hazard** – e.g. light engineering and assembly work, food processing warehousing, extensive work with dangerous machinery or sharp instruments, construction, chemical manufacture etc | Less than 5 | 1 Small Kit |
| | 5-25 | 1 Medium Kit |
| | More than 25 | 1 Large Kit per 25 employees |

Special circumstances also need to be considered such as remoteness from medical services, special hazards such as the use of hydrofluoric acid and sites with several buildings. In these situations there may need to be more first aid kits than set out in the table.

## British Standard Compliant First Aid Kit Contents

| Contents | Small | Medium | Large | Contents | Small | Medium | Large |
|---|---|---|---|---|---|---|---|
| First Aid Guidance Leaflet | 1 | 1 | 1 | HypaPlast Microporous Tape, 2.5cm x 5m | 1 | 1 | 1 |
| HypaCover First Aid Dressings, 12x12cm | 4 | 6 | 8 | HypaTouch Nitrile Gloves (Pair) | 6 | 9 | 12 |
| HypaCover First Aid Dressings, 18x18cm | 1 | 2 | 2 | HypaCover Finger Dressings | 2 | 3 | 4 |
| HypaBand Triangular Bandages | 2 | 3 | 4 | HypaGuard Face Shields | 1 | 1 | 2 |
| HypaBand Safety Pins | 12 | 12 | 24 | HypaGuard Foil Blankets | 1 | 2 | 3 |
| HypaCover Eye Dressings | 2 | 3 | 4 | Burn Dressings, 10x10cm | 1 | 2 | 2 |
| HypaPlast Washproof Plasters | 40 | 60 | 100 | Clothing Cutters | 1 | 1 | 1 |
| HypaClean Sterile Wipes | 20 | 30 | 40 | HypaBand Conforming Bandages, 7.5cm | 1 | 2 | 2 |

## Additional First Aid Supplies

The contents table provides a minimum guidance for what should be included in a workplace first aid kit. Employers are required to conduct a risk assessment of the working environment to identify risks that may require additional first aid items to be provided.

These requirements may change where there are differing levels of risk within the workplace. An example of differing risks would be where a workplace has office space and also factory space.

## Eyewash

In the workplace, eyewash should be provided where there is no easy access to running water.

The HSE indicates that "if mains tap water is not readily available for eye irrigation, at least one litre of sterile water or sterile normal saline (0.9%) in sealed, disposable containers should be provided. Once the seal has been broken, containers should not be kept for reuse. Containers should not be used beyond their expiry date."

## Maintaining First Aid Supplies

All first aid supplies should be checked on a regular basis to ensure that first aid kits remain fully stocked and all items remain within their expiry date. This practice is essential to ensure that first aid kits are ready for use when they are needed.

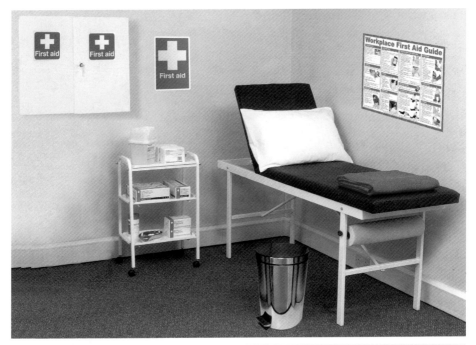

## First Aid Room

The Health & Safety (First Aid) Regulations 1981 states "Employers should provide a suitable first aid room or rooms where the assessment of first aid needs identifies this as necessary.

The first aid room(s) should contain essential first aid facilities and equipment, be easily accessible to stretchers and clearly signposted and identified.

If possible the room(s) should be reserved exclusively for giving first aid."

### First Aid Room:

+ First Aid Couch
+ First Aid Room Sign
+ First Aid Guidance Poster
+ Trolley, 3 Tier
+ Blanket, Scarlet Cotton
+ Polyester Filled Pillow
+ Metal Cabinet
+ Pedal Bin
+ Economy Couch Roll

## Transporting A Casualty

When transporting a casualty several factors need to be taken into consideration. You need to think about the casualty, the environment and yourself.

### What should I consider?

**The casualty:**

+ Do you have to move the casualty?
+ Can you move them without endangering yourself or the casualty?
+ Will the casualty be able to help you?
+ Are there enough people to help you carry the casualty plus look after them?
+ Do you need to transport them home or to hospital?

**The environment:**

+ What equipment do you have?
+ Is it suitable for the task?
+ Do you know how to use it?
+ Is the area clear to transport the casualty?
+ Is the walking surface suitable for transporting a casualty?

**Yourself:**

+ Are you fit enough?
+ Are you trained in lifting and handling?
+ Is there anyone to help you?

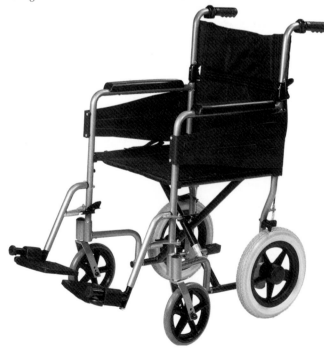

# 02 First Aid Principles

This section introduces you to the principles of first aid and how to approach a casualty. It identifies factors that help you assess the situation, how to prioritise your actions, delegate bystanders and summon help or the emergency medical services (EMS).

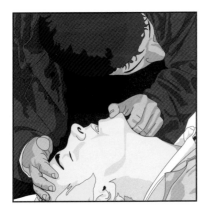

## Content

# First Aid Principles

## Definition Of First Aid

First aid is the immediate help or treatment of a person following an accident, illness or injury. The first aider may then give appropriate treatment, advice, refer the patient to casualty, their General Practitioner or summon the emergency medical services.

## Aims & Objectives Of A First Aider

The aims of a first aider are to:

+ Understand your own abilities and limitations.
+ Keep yourself and all others safe and calm at all times.
+ Assess the situation quickly and calmly.
+ Summon help quickly if needed or necessary.
+ Assess the casualty. Provide treatment if necessary.
+ Summon EMS, pass on all information.
+ Seek help yourself if needed. Remember your needs.

## Hygiene

To protect yourself and others from infections use and carry the following Protective Equipment:

+ Nitrile gloves.
+ Face shield for CPR.
+ Clinical waste bag.
+ Hand gel to clean hands.

## Infection Control

Before, during and after administering first aid, it is important that you protect yourself and the casualty from the spread of infection. Infection can enter the body through a break in the skin, mucous membranes (mouth, eyes, and nose) and inhalation. When treating a wound there is a risk that blood-borne viruses can be transmitted. These include Hepatitis B, Hepatitis C and Human Immunodeficiency Virus (HIV). If simple protection and hygiene precautions are taken, the risk of infection is **very low** and this should not stop you carrying out first aid.

+ Do not use bare hands when dealing with a wound.
+ Always wear disposable gloves (latex-free).
+ Use a face shield during CPR.
+ Cover any open wounds you may have with waterproof dressings.
+ Wash hands thoroughly.
+ Use hand gel to clean hands.
+ Do not cough, breathe or sneeze over a wound.
+ Use a plastic disposable apron if dealing with body fluid.
+ Dispose of clinical waste safely.

If you are worried you have been exposed to infection while giving first aid, seek medical advice immediately.

## How To Wash Hands

01. Wet hands with water and apply soap or handwash.

02. Rub hands palm to palm.

03. Rub palm over the back of the other hand with interlaced fingers and vice versa.

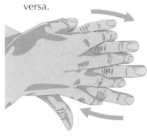

04. Palm to palm with fingers interlaced.

05. Back of fingers to opposing palms with fingers interlocked.

06. Rotational rubbing of left thumb clasped in right palm and vice versa.

07. Rotational rubbing, backwards and forwards with clasped fingers of right hand in left palm and vice versa.

08. Rinse hands under running warm water.

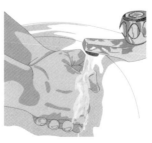

09. Dry hand thoroughly with a paper towel or air dryer.

10. Use your elbow or paper towel to turn off the tap.

# First Aid Principles

## Priority Of Injuries

There is a recognised protocol for prioritising injuries.

### Danger

Be aware of your own and the casualty's safety and remove the danger as safely as possible. For example ensuring that there are no chemical or electrical hazards, and that any machinery is turned off.

### Response (AVPU)

| A | Alert |
| V | Verbal |
| P | Pain |
| U | Unresponsive |

Check whether the casualty is responsive. A mild pain stimulus should also be applied at this stage, which may cause the casualty to respond. Using a system known as **AVPU**.

Check whether the casualty is responsive. Extra care is required with casualties who may have a neck or spinal injury.

### Alert

Call to the casualty as you approach them to see if they respond.

### Verbal

Ask "Open your eyes if you can hear me."

### Pain

Offer a mild pain stimulus by shaking casualty's shoulders to see if the casualty responds at all.

### Unresponsive

If the casualty does not respond to any of the above. They should be deemed to be unresponsive.

## The ABC Of Resuscitation

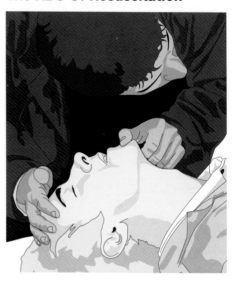

The following priorities are discussed in more detail in later sections:

| A | Airway |
| B | Breathing |
| C | Circulation |

Once you have established that basic life support is not required.

### Then look for other injuries such as:

+ Life threatening bleeding.
+ Head and spinal injuries.
+ Burns and poisoning.
+ Fractures and dislocations.
+ Minor wounds and soft tissue injuries.

### Priority of injuries

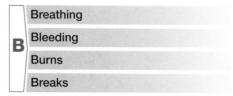

| B | Breathing |
| | Bleeding |
| | Burns |
| | Breaks |

## Multiple Casualties

When there are multiple casualties it is often difficult to decide who to attend to first. If any casualties appear unresponsive or lifeless they are the first to be attended to.

If there are two or more casualties who appear unresponsive attend to those who are on their backs first, as their airway is more likely to be blocked than those who are on their front or side.

## Calling For Assistance

If there are other people around, call for help once you realise that emergency services will be required.

Some companies have their own local policy for calling the emergency services such as phoning the security department or reception.

It is important that you are aware of your local policy. When calling the emergency services remember to tell them:

+ Location of the casualty.
+ Number of casualties.
+ Type of injury and if casualty is breathing or not.
+ Any hazard, for example a chemical that might require breathing apparatus.
+ On a large site which entrance to use.

If the site is large, ensure reception is aware that the emergency services are on their way. Send bystanders to escort the emergency services to the location of the casualty.

**If the casualty is not breathing, ask for an AED (Automated External Defibrillator).**

## Consent

You must get consent from a casualty before starting treatment.

If the casualty refuses to give consent, inform emergency medical services.

If the casualty is unresponsive, consent can be assumed.

# 03 Assessing a Casualty

When assessing a casualty you need to identify and deal with any life threatening conditions or injuries by conducting a **Primary Survey**.

If there are no life threatening injuries or they have been successfully managed you carry on the assessment and perform a **Secondary Survey**.

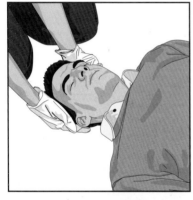

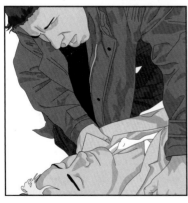

## Content

## Primary Survey

### What is a Primary Survey?

The primary survey is an initial step by step assessment of a casualty to identify life threatening conditions or injuries. By following the sequences of the survey, conditions and injuries can be dealt with in order of priority. When conducting the survey you should not move on to the next step unless the current step has been completed or successfully treated.

The primary survey must be conducted on every casualty you treat. It is essential you are not distracted by other events whilst conducting the primary survey.

### DANGER

Assess the danger, any hazards to yourself or casualty?

### RESPONSE

Using AVPU
**A**lert, **V**erbal, **P**ain & **U**nresponsive.

### AIRWAY

Check their mouth for any obvious obstruction, perform the chin lift head tilt.

### BREATHING

Look for their chest movement. Listen for breathing sound. Feel their breath. All for 10 seconds.

**NO**

### CALL 999/112

Call for ambulance immediately.

### DEFIBRILLATION

Ask for AED if available.

### START CPR

Compress chest 30 times at rate of 100-120 compressions per minutes. 2 Rescue breaths, blow in for 1 second, 2 breaths within 5 seconds. Repeat 30 chest compressions.

**YES**

### CALL 999/112

Call for ambulance immediately.

### SECONDARY SURVEY

Carry out secondary survey.

### RECOVERY POSITION

Place casualty in recovery position.

### CIRCULATION

Are there any severe bleeds which may lead to shock?

## Airway

### What is an airway?

The airway is the mouth, nose, and trachea (windpipe). In an unresponsive casualty the relaxed muscles can allow the tongue to fall backwards and block the airway.

The airway also becomes blocked when someone chokes.

### What should I do?

+ Place one hand on the casualty's forehead and gently tilt their head back. As you do this the mouth will fall open slightly.

+ Place the fingertips of your other hand on the point of their chin and lift their chin.

+ Look inside the mouth for any obvious obstructions.

## Secondary Survey

### What is a Secondary Survey?

Once the primary survey is completed and you have dealt with any life threatening conditions you can perform the secondary survey to check for other injuries by performing the head-to-toe examination.

If the casualty is responsive or there is a family member or friend around them, try to find out:

+ **History** - What actually happened and any relevant medical history.

+ **Signs** - Injuries or abnormalities that you can see.

+ **Symptoms** - Injuries or abnormalities that the casualty tells you about.

## History (AMPLE)

### What is History?

The events leading up to the casualty calling for assistance may help indicate the condition that requires first aid assistance.

For example, a person who states they are a diabetic, feeling unwell and have missed a meal due to a meeting, probably indicates that a sugar drink is required as the first aid action.

| A | Allergy |
|---|---|
| M | Medications |
| P | Previous medical history |
| L | Last meal |
| E | Event history |

There may be other clues such as tablets or inhalers near to the casualty indicating to the first aider that the casualty has a specific illness or conditions.

### What should I do?

01. Find out what happened from casualty or people around.

02. Look for other clues which can indicate the likely nature of the casualty's injury.

03. Ask about AMPLE.

04. Note the presence of a medical warning bracelet which may indicate an on going medical condition.

## Signs

### What are Signs?

These are clues that the first aider sees, hears, feels or smells. For example you may see sweating, hear wheezy breathing, feel a fast pulse, smell alcohol. These signs will assist you in your first aid response.

### What should I do?

01. Observe and feel casualty for swelling, bleeding, discolouration, deformity and smells.
02. Use all your senses, look, listen, feel and smell.
03. Compare the injured side of the body to the uninjured side and take note if casualty is unable to perform normal functions such as moving limbs or standing.
04. Make a note of any obvious superficial injuries and treat them only once you have completed the examination.

## Symptoms

### What are Symptoms?

The casualty may describe how they feel. These symptoms may suggest a particular course of action for the first aider. Symptoms may include phrases such as "I feel sick"; "I'm in pain."

### What should I do?

01. Get casualty to describe sensations that they feel, such as pain.
02. Ask where they feel it, and what makes it better or worse such as movements.
03. Did it result from injury? If not then where and how it began.
04. Listen and take notes on all the symptoms described by the casualty.

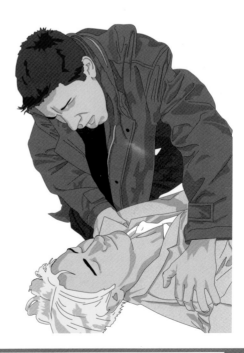

## Head to Toe Examination On An Unresponsive Casualty

What should I do?

01. Assess breathing, check rate, depth and nature.

02. Start with examining the casualty's head, run hands over scalp to feel for bleeding, swelling or depression which may indicate fracture.

    **DO NOT** move casualty if you suspect an injured neck. *See fig.1*

*Fig.1*

03. Look for clear fluid or watery blood from ear as these may be signs of a serious head injury.

04. Examine eyes and note if they are open.

    Check the pupil size, if they are not the same it may indicate head injury.

    Look for any foreign object, blood, or bruising in the whites of the eyes.

05. Check the nose for discharge as you did for the ears.

*Fig.2*

06. Look at the skin, note colour and temperature; look out for blue tinge on lips, ears and face.

07. Loosen clothing around the neck and look for medical alerts *See fig.2* or stoma fitted.

    Run your fingers gently along the spine from the base of the skull down as far as possible without moving the casualty. Check for irregularity, swelling, tenderness or deformity.

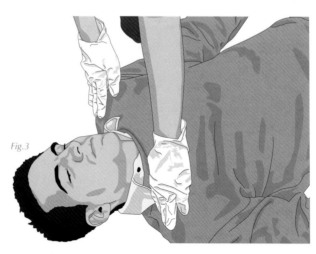

*Fig.3*

08. Look at the chest to note whether the chest expands evenly, easily and equally on both sides.

Feel the rib cage to check for deformity, irregularity or tenderness.

09. Feel along the collar bones, shoulders, upper arms, elbows, hands and fingers for any swelling, tenderness or deformity. *See fig.3*

Check the casualty has no abnormal sensations in the arms or fingers.

If the finger tips are pale or grey-blue, there may be a problem with blood circulation.

10. If there is any impairment in movement or loss of sensation in the limbs.

**DO NOT** move the casualty to examine the spine.

11. Gently feel the casualty's abdomen to detect any evidence of bleeding and to identify any rigidity or tenderness of the muscular wall which could be a sign of internal bleeding. *See fig.4*

12. Check the legs. Look and feel for bleeding, swelling, deformity or tenderness.

Check the movement and feeling in the toes.

13. Check that the casualty has no abnormal sensations in their feet or toes. *See fig.5*

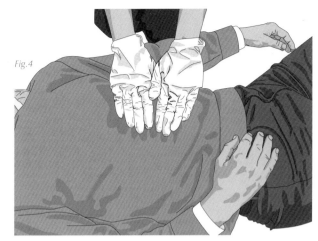

*Fig.4*

*Fig.5*

# 04 The Unresponsive Casualty

This section looks at the common causes of asphyxia and describes how to maintain a casualty's airway. It shows how to recognise when there are problems with the breathing and the circulation and how to respond to these situations. It goes on to discuss the causes and management of an unresponsive casualty.

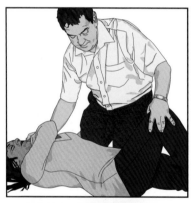

## Content

## The Unresponsive Casualty

What is Unresponsiveness?

Unresponsiveness is where the brain's normal activity has been interrupted.

The human body needs an adequate supply of oxygen to enter the lungs in order to oxygenate the blood. This oxygenated blood is then pumped around the body to transfer oxygen to all the cells in the body.

If a person is deprived of oxygen for any length of time, the brain will begin to fail. As a result, the casualty will eventually lose responsiveness, breathing will cease, the heart will stop and death results.

The main causes are:

+ Fainting
+ Infection (Extremes of Temperature)
+ Shock
+ Heart Attack
+ Stroke

+ Asphyxia (low blood oxygen – hypoxia)
+ Poisoning
  (e.g. chemicals, alcohol or drug intoxication)
+ Seizures
+ Diabetes
+ Head Injury

### DANGER

Assess the danger, any hazards to yourself or casualty?

### AIRWAY

Check their mouth for any obvious obstruction, perform the chin lift head tilt.

**NO**

### RESPONSE

Check if they respond to your voice. Shake their shoulders gently.

**YES**

### MONITOR

Monitor and record vital signs i.e. level of response, breathing and pulse.

### BREATHING

Look for their chest movement. Listen for breathing sound. Feel their breath. All for 10 seconds.

### CIRCULATION

Are there any severe bleeds which may lead to shock?

### CALL 999/112

Call for ambulance immediately.

## The Recovery Position

### What is the Recovery Position?

The recovery position is used when a casualty is unresponsive and breathing. The recovery position allows the head to be placed tilted back and down. This stops the tongue from blocking the airway and will allow any vomit and fluid to drain from the mouth.

The main aim of the Recovery Position is to ensure that the casualty is:

+ Stable, to prevent the casualty falling out of the position if you have to leave.
+ They are on their side.
+ Their head is be positioned to maintain the airway but secretions or vomit can drain away.
+ There is no pressure on the chest that restricts breathing.
+ They can be turned easily and safely onto their back.
+ The casualty can be positioned quickly for CPR.

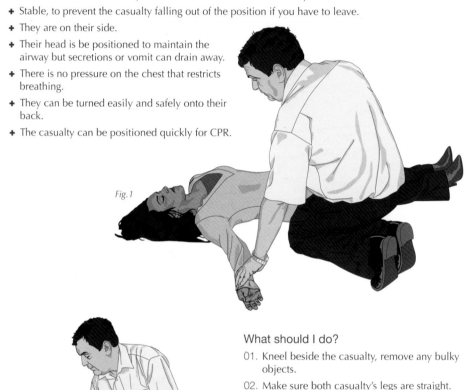

*Fig.1*

*Fig.2*

### What should I do?

01. Kneel beside the casualty, remove any bulky objects.

02. Make sure both casualty's legs are straight.

Place the arm that is nearest to you at right angles to the casualty's body with the elbow bent and the palm facing upwards. *See fig.1*

03. Bring the arm that is furthest from you across the casualty's chest and hold back their hand against the cheek nearest to you. *See fig.2*

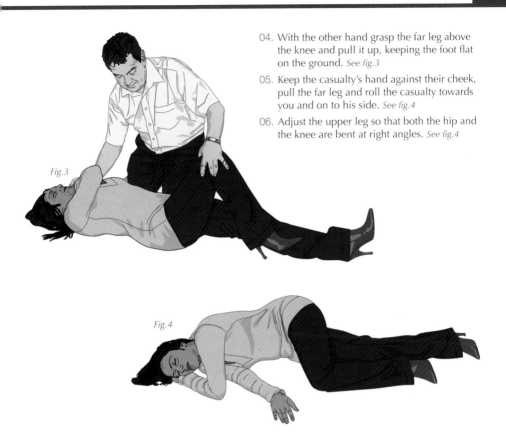

04. With the other hand grasp the far leg above the knee and pull it up, keeping the foot flat on the ground. *See fig.3*

05. Keep the casualty's hand against their cheek, pull the far leg and roll the casualty towards you and on to his side. *See fig.4*

06. Adjust the upper leg so that both the hip and the knee are bent at right angles. *See fig.4*

Fig.3

Fig.4

07. Tilt the casualty's head back and tilt their chin so that the airway remains open. *See fig.5*

08. Alert the Emergency Medical Services (EMS) by calling 999/112, if not already done so. Get an AED if available. Monitor and record vital signs, breathing pulse, level of response and temperature.

09. If the casualty has been left in the recovery position for longer than 30 minutes, roll them on their back and then roll them on the opposite side - unless other injuries prevent you from doing so.

Fig.5

## Cardiopulmonary Resuscitation (CPR)

### What is Cardiopulmonary Resuscitation?

Cardiopulmonary resuscitation (CPR) is a procedure performed to sustain the life of a casualty in cardiac arrest. By delivering CPR the first aider is manually oxygenating and pumping the casualty's blood to preserve brain function.

CPR should be conducted until either further measures can be taken to restore heart function, such as using a defibrillator or the heart functionality is restored through delivering CPR.

If you have not had any former training in CPR, just do compressions only, no rescue breaths.

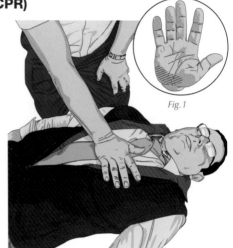

Fig.1

### What should I do?

01. Ensure the casualty is on a firm, flat surface.

02. Place the heel of one hand on top of the other in the centre of the casualty's chest.
    *See fig.1*

03. Compress the chest (up to a maximum depth of approximately 5-6cm) 30 times at a rate of 100-120 compressions per minute. The compressions and releases should take an equal amount of time.

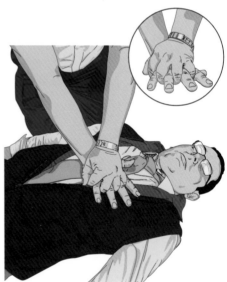

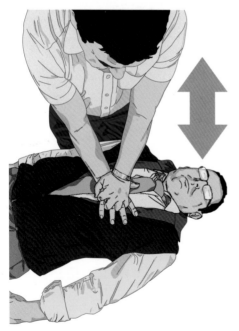

04. After 30 compressions, open the airway again using head tilt/chin lift. *See fig.2*

05. Seal the nostrils with your thumb and forefinger.

06. Blow into the mouth, 2 effective rescue breaths in total. (Blow in for 1 second, 2 breaths within 10 seconds). *See fig.3*

07. Remove your mouth to the side and inhale some fresh air, when breathing for the casualty.

08. Repeat so you have given 2 effective rescue breaths in total within 10 seconds.

09. Go back to 30 compressions then try again with 2 breaths.

10. Return your hands to the correct position on the chest and give a further 30 chest compressions.

## Continue with CPR until

+ The casualty shows signs of recovery.

+ Emergency services arrive.

+ You become exhausted and unable to continue.

+ The situation changes and you are now in immediate danger.

## Seizures

Seizure like episodes can occur following a cardiac arrest. If in doubt start CPR.

*Fig.2*

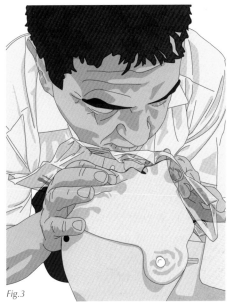

*Fig.3*

## Automated External Defibrillator (AED)

### What is an Automated External Defibrillator?

AEDs are safe, reliable and sophisticated computerised machines that deliver shocks to a casualty that has suffered a cardiac arrest. Semi-automatic and Automatic AEDs work by analysing the victim's heart rhythm to determine the need for a shock. Cardiac arrest occurs when the heart stops beating, resulting in blood not being pumped around the body. Following a cardiac arrest it is essential to act quickly and use an AED. Semi-automatic and automatic AEDs can be used by untrained personnel because they provide full step by step guidance for preparing the casualty and will only allow a shock to be given to a casualty if it is needed.

The chance of survival following a cardiac arrest reduces by 14% every minute that passes. (British Heart Foundation)

### What should I do?

01. Switch on the AED and follow the voice prompts.

02. Prompts will ask you if the emergency services have been called.

03. Remove the pads from the sealed packet and place onto the casualty's bare chest, follow the diagrams on the pads for placement.

04. Once both pads are on the casualty it will ask you to make sure that nobody is touching the casualty whilst it analyses for a shockable rhythm.

05. If the casualty requires a shock the AED will now charge up.

    To deliver a shock press the shock button when prompted.

06. After a shock has been delivered the AED will prompt you that it is safe to touch the casualty, it will prompt you to start CPR and full instructions will be given by the AED.

    Start CPR for 2 minutes, after 2 minutes the AED will reanalyse the heart rhythm and may deliver further shocks if required.

07. Don't stop until either a trained First Aider or Emergency services arrive or the casualty shows signs of recovery.

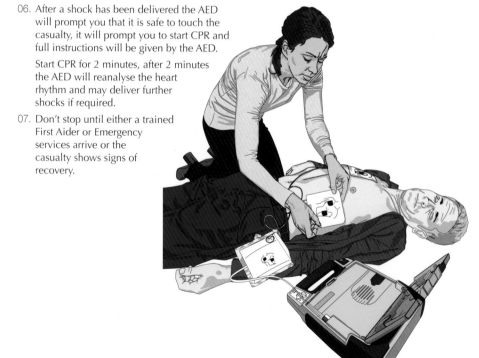

# 05 Respiratory Problems

This section looks at the common causes of asphyxia and describes how to maintain a casualty's airway. It shows how to recognise when there are problems with the breathing and the circulation and how to respond to these situations. It goes on to discuss the causes and management of an unresponsive casualty.

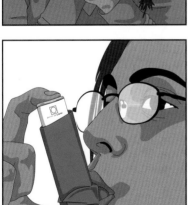

## Content

## Respiratory System

### What is the respiratory system?

The respiratory system comprises of the nose, mouth, trachea (windpipe), bronchus, and bronchioles, which lead to the alveolar sacs in the lungs.

Breathing is controlled by the nervous system. The brain monitors the level of oxygen and carbon dioxide in the blood and controls the rate of breathing.

The diaphragm contracts and the pressure within the chest cavity decreases thus sucking the air into the lungs.

The oxygen is transferred to the circulatory system in the alveoli via a process called gaseous exchange.

Carbon dioxide is removed from the blood via the alveoli in the lungs and breathed out through the air passages.

## Airway

### What is an airway?

The airway is the mouth, nose, and trachea (windpipe). In an unresponsive casualty the relaxed muscles can allow the tongue to fall backwards and block the airway.

The airway also becomes blocked when someone chokes.

### How do I recognise a blocked airway?

+ Noisy breathing.
+ Blue tinge to the skin and lips (cyanosis).

### What should I do?

01. Look into the mouth and remove any obvious obstruction.

02. If it is caused by the tongue this can be corrected easily by lifting the chin with two fingers of one hand and at the same time placing the other hand on the casualty's forehead and gently tilting the head back. This is known as chin lift head tilt. *See Fig.1*

03. Once the airway has been cleared, check for breathing.

*Fig.1*

## Asphyxia / Hypoxia

### What is asphyxia / hypoxia?

This is when there is difficulty in breathing leading to low oxygen levels in the blood. There are several causes, the main ones being:

+ Insufficient oxygen in the air e.g. some chemical spills.

+ Obstruction of the airway e.g. by the tongue obstructing the airway in an unresponsive casualty.

+ Injury to the chest wall preventing breathing e.g. following a fall, or a crush injury.

+ Lung disease e.g. asthma.

+ Airway swelling e.g. anaphylaxis or burns.

+ Inability of the blood to carry oxygen e.g. carbon monoxide poisoning.

+ Damage to the central nervous system e.g. following a head injury.

### How do I recognise asphyxia / hypoxia?

+ Noisy breathing / flaring nostrils.

+ Accessory muscle movement trying to use neck and shoulder muscles to assist breathing.

+ Grey / blue skin and lips (cyanosis).

+ Agitation / confusion / anxiety.

### Causes of asphyxia / hypoxia

+ Asthma

+ Choking

+ Anaphylaxis

## Asthma

### What is asthma?

This is where the muscles of the airway go into spasm, swell and become blocked with mucus plugs. A trigger for an asthma attack can be allergy, infection, emotional or environmental factors.

### How do I recognise asthma?

+ A known history of asthma.

+ Difficulty in breathing.

+ An audible wheeze.

+ Distress or anxiety.

+ Coughing and difficulty in speaking.

+ Blue tinge to skin (cyanosis).

+ Exhaustion.

### What should I do?

01. Sit the casualty in a comfortable position that does not restrict chest expansion.

02. Try to get casualty to calm their breathing down first.

03. The casualty will usually have a blue (reliever) inhaler with them. Assist the casualty to take this. If this has not helped in few minutes, call 999/112 for emergency help.

04. Stay calm.

05. If the attack is relieved encourage the person to inform their doctor of this attack.

## Choking

### What is choking?

Choking occurs when an object such as food, sweets or small objects become lodged in the airway blocking the passage of air from the mouth and nose to the lungs.

### How do I recognise choking?

+ Difficult laboured or absent breathing.
+ Facial features, look of fear, quick colour change, eyes widen and water, leaning forward and clutching throat.

### What should I do?

**In a responsive casualty**

01. Lean the casualty forwards and encourage them to cough.
02. Perform up to 5 back blows in between their shoulder blades.
03. If this does not dislodge the blockage perform up to 5 abdominal thrusts by standing behind the casualty and placing your fist below where the ribs meet and pull inwards and upwards.
04. Continue with 5 back slaps, 5 abdominal thrusts until the blockage is dislodged or until medical help arrives.
05. Call the EMS (999/112) after 1 cycle of back blows and abdominal thrusts.

**In an unresponsive casualty**

01. If casualty is not breathing, immediately call for the emergency services.
02. Begin CPR (Cardio Pulmonary Resuscitation).
03. Begin chest compressions to dislodge the obstruction, give up to 30 compressions and then check the mouth.
04. Attempt two rescue breaths. Each rescue breath should be 1 second and 2 in 10 seconds.
05. If the chest does not rise or breathing has not returned to normal, give another 30 chest compressions.
06. Continue CPR cycles until obstruction has been removed or the emergency services arrive and take over.

### For all choking casualties

+ Assess breathing even after the blockage appears to have been removed.
+ Seek further medical advice.

### DO NOT give abdominal thrust if:

+ a baby under 1 year old
+ a pregnant woman

## Anaphylactic Shock

What is anaphylactic shock?

Anaphylaxis is a severe allergic reaction at the extreme end of the allergic response range.

The whole body is affected, usually within minutes of exposure to the allergen but sometimes it can take longer for the reaction to show.

What are the most common causes?

+ Peanuts/nuts
+ Sesame
+ Fish/shellfish
+ Dairy Products/eggs

+ Wasp/bee stings
+ Latex
+ Penicillin
+ Other drugs/injections

How do I recognise anaphylactic shock?

+ Swelling in the throat and mouth.
+ Difficulty in swallowing and/or speaking.
+ Alterations in the heart rate.
+ Difficulty in breathing (due to severe asthma or throat swelling).
+ Hives (often large) appear on the body.
+ Generalised flushing of the skin.
+ Abdominal cramps, nausea and vomiting.
+ Sudden feeling of weakness/faint – due to a drop in blood pressure.
+ Possible sense of impending doom.
+ Collapse and unresponsiveness.

Fig. 1

What should I do?

01. Your first step is to dial 999/112 – do not hesitate.

02. Place casualty in a sitting position (making it easier for them to breath).

03. Help the casualty to sit up in the position that best relieves any breathing difficulty. If becomes pale with a weak pulse, help them to lie down with legs raised and treat for shock.

04. Monitor and record vital signs while waiting for help to arrive.

05. Adrenaline is the first line of defence. An adrenaline (epinephrine) injection commonly known as the auto injectors must be given, as prescribed, as soon as serious reaction is suspected. See fig.1

06. Massage the area for 10 seconds after injections.

07. Give second auto injector 5 minutes after first one if no improvement.

Both Jext and Epipen auto-injectors are approved for use in the UK by NICE (National Institute for Health and Care Excellence).

# 06 Managing External & Internal Bleeding

This section discusses arterial and venous external bleeding and how to manage casualties who are bleeding. It defines internal bleeding and how the first aider may recognise someone who is bleeding internally. Different wound types are explained and the action required by the first aider when presented with different types of wounds.

## Content

## External Bleeding

What types of bleeding are there?

Bleeding from any source can look dramatic, however this should not distract you from checking essential things first such as the airway and breathing. Bleeding can come from arteries, veins, and capillaries.

+ **Arterial bleeding** - Arteries have thick muscular walls and carry oxygen - rich blood. The blood is usually bright red and pulsates. This type of bleeding can rapidly reduce blood volume leading to hypovolaemic shock.

+ **Venous bleeding** - Veins carry blood which carries the carbon dioxide. The blood flows rather than pulsates, as it is under less pressure than arterial blood, and appears darker. A casualty can still loose a lot of blood from a severed major vein.

+ **Capillary bleeding** - Capillaries are single layered vessels. Bleeding from capillaries seeps quickly at first but then slows and clots.

## Managing Different Wound Types

What types of wounds are there?

Different types of wounds cause different types of bleeding or situations for the first aider to assess.

### Major wounds

These can be incisions where the wound has clean sharp edges or lacerations where the wound edges are ragged. Deep puncture wounds can damage deep structures and can contain debris.

Gunshot wounds can have both an entrance and exit site with damage along the missile tract. Other structures such as tendons may also be damaged in a major wound.

### Minor wounds

These are more superficial but can be serious as they may hide damaged structures underneath the wound.

These can be abrasions, which often contain foreign bodies, or bruising where a blow damages capillaries beneath the skin, which may hide a fracture or internal injury.

## Recognition Of Wounds

### Abrasion

A superficial wound to the skin where the skin has been scraped away. These are often caused by friction or rubbing and are commonly known as a graze or scrape. Fibres can become embedded in to abrasions which can lead to infection.

### Incision

A serious cut made in to the skin or flesh usually caused by a sharp object e.g. a knife. Incisions are usually deep with smooth edges and lead to substantial blood loss as they often cut across blood vessels.

### Laceration

A cut or tear to the skin that can often be quite deep, often of an irregular or jagged shape. A laceration will not tend to bleed as much as an incision but do tend to be contaminated by the object that caused the cut and can lead to infection.

### Puncture

A puncture wound is usually a narrow but deep wound caused by an object piercing the skin creating a hole. These are often caused by standing on an object like a nail causing bacteria to enter the wound which can result in infection.

## Major Wounds

What should I do?

01. Check for danger, response, airway, breathing and circulation. Protect yourself by using gloves or other improvised barrier for protection.

02. Sit them down.

03. Expose the wound by removing or cutting off clothing.

04. Inspect the wound for foreign bodies.

05. Apply direct pressure over the wound to stop the bleeding.

06. Apply an appropriately sized first aid dressing over the wound. If there is an object in the wound do not remove it but pack around it.

07. Secure the dressing still applying pressure if required. If blood seeps through this dressing apply a second one on top of the first.

    If blood continues to seep through, remove both dressings, relocate wound and apply a fresh dressing, ensuring pressure is applied accurately to point of bleeding.

08. Observe for the signs of hypovolaemic shock and treat if necessary.

## Minor Wounds, Cuts & Grazes

What should I do?

01. Check for danger, response, airway, breathing and circulation; protect yourself by using gloves or other improvised barrier for protection.

02. Expose the wound and stop any bleeding by using pressure and a first aid dressing as above.

    Do not proceed to cleaning or dressing the wound unless you have stopped the bleeding.

03. If there is debris in the wound dousing it in sterile wound cleaning fluid can flush this out or tap water can be used.

04. Apply a sterile non-adhesive dressing or plaster as appropriate.

05. Check if there is an underlying injury for example a soft tissue injury or fracture.

06. Advise the casualty to seek further medical advice if either the first aider or the casualty is concerned.

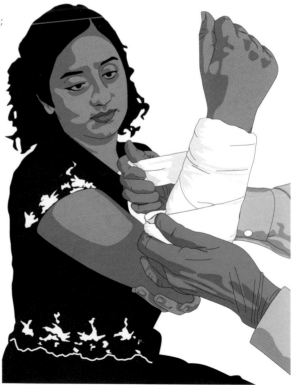

## Penetrating Chest Wound

### What is a penetrating chest wound?

Something sharp has penetrated the chest wall this can lead to severe damage to organs and abdomen which will lead to shock. Lungs are susceptible to injury, either by damage to themselves or from wounds that perforate the two layered membrane that surrounds and protects the lungs. Air can enter between the membrane and exert pressure on the lung, which may cause the lung to collapse.

### How do I recognise a penetrating chest wound?

+ Rapid and shallow breathing
+ Difficult and painful breathing
+ Pale Clammy skin
+ Coughing up frothy red blood
+ Blood bubbling out of the wound
+ Sound of air being sucked into the chest
+ A crackling feeling of the skin around the site of the wound

### What should I do?

01. Leave open to environment.
02. Call 999 /112 for an ambulance.
03. Treat for shock.
04. If unresponsive place in the recovery position injured side down.
05. Monitor and record.

## Internal Bleeding

### What is internal bleeding?

Within the body there are large cavities which can fill with blood following an injury which damages an internal structure. This can cause a significant loss of circulating blood. With internal bleeding there is usually a history of trauma for example, a blow to the abdomen or back.

Although no bleeding is usually apparent, there will be symptoms of loosing circulatory blood volume. This is called Hypovolaemic shock.

### How do I recognise internal bleeding?

Possible sign of internal bleeding, may be visible signs of bleeding from body orifices.

+ Anus or vagina - will be bright red mixed with mucus
+ Ear or nose - will be bright red, may be accompanied by clear fluid.
+ Bleeding from lungs - casualty will cough up frothy blood and coffee coloured grains
+ Urinary tract - results will be red or dark smoky coloured urine

### What should I do?

01. Call 999 /112 for an ambulance.
02. If responsive lie down, elevate legs or bend at the knees.
03. If unresponsive place in the recovery position.
04. Loosen tight clothing.
05. Protect from the environment, keep warm.
06. Monitor and record levels of responsiveness.
07. Look for markers i.e. seat belt bruising signs of internal bleeding.

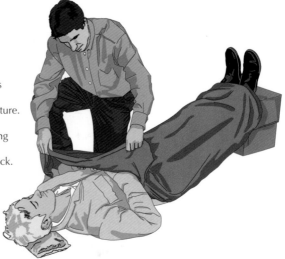

## Hypovolaemic Shock

### What is Hypovolaemic shock?

Hyovolaemic shock is a life threatening condition and should be given top priority treatment.

It is caused when the circulatory system is disturbed and fails. Results in the organs of the body being subjected to oxygen starvation.

The most common cause is when the body loses blood greater then 2 litres (3.5 pints) from external or internal bleeding.

### How do I recognise Hypovolaemic shock?

+ Apparent external bleeding or a history which indicates possible internal bleeding.
+ Pale, cold, clammy skin
+ Rapid weak pulse
+ Rapid shallow breathing, anxiety, confusion and agitation
+ Restlessness
+ Collapse
+ Unresponsiveness
+ Thirst

### What should I do?

01. Check for danger, response, airway, breathing and circulation.
02. Lie the casualty down and raise and support legs, unless there is a back injury.
03. Loosen clothing around the neck. *See fig.1*
04. Call for the emergency medical services.
05. Monitor and record breathing, pulse and responsiveness level.
06. Place in the recovery position if the casualty becomes unresponsive.
07. Reassure the casualty at all times.
08. Stay with the casualty until help arrives.
09. Nil by mouth.
10. Moisten lips with water.

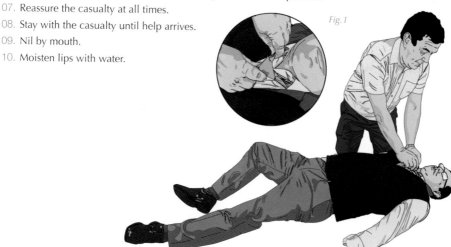

*Fig. 1*

## Bleeding Varicose Vein

### What is a bleeding varicose vein?

Veins contain one-way valves that keep the blood flowing towards the heart. If these valves fail, blood collects (pools) behind them and makes the veins swell. This problem, called varicose veins, usually develops in the legs.

A varicose vein has taut, thin walls and is often raised, typically producing knobbly skin over the affected area. The vein can be burst by a gentle knock, and this may result in profuse bleeding. Shock will quickly develop if bleeding is not controlled.

### What should I do?

01. Lie the casualty on their back. Raise and support the injured leg as high as possible.

02. Apply firm, direct pressure on to the injury, using a sterile dressing, or a clean, non-fluffy pad, until the bleed is under control. If necessary, carefully cut away clothing to expose the site of the bleeding.

03. Remove garments such as garters or elastic-topped stockings because these may cause the bleeding to continue.

04. Keeping the leg raised, put another large, soft pad over the dressing. Bandage it firmly enough to exert even pressure, but not so tightly that the circulation in the limb is impaired.

05. Call 999/112 for emergency help. Keep the injured leg raised and supported until the ambulance arrives. Monitor and record vital signs - level of response, breathing and pulse regularly until help arrives. In addition, check the circulation in the limb beyond the bandage every 10 minutes.

## Nosebleed

### What is a nosebleed?

Bleeding from the nose most commonly occurs when tiny blood vessels inside the nostrils are ruptured. Nosebleeds may also occur as a result of high blood pressure and anti-clotting medication.

If bleeding follows a head injury, the blood may appear thin and watery. This is a very serious sign because it indicates that the skull is fractured and fluid is leaking from around the brain.

### What should I do?

01. Tell the casualty to sit down and tilt their head forward. Ask casualty to breathe through their mouth and to pinch the soft part of their nose for up to ten minutes.

02. Advise the casualty not to speak, swallow, cough, spit or sniff since this may disturb blood clots that have formed in the nose. Give them a clean cloth or tissue to mop up any dribbling.

03. After ten minutes, tell the casualty to release the pressure. If the bleeding has not stopped, tell them to reapply the pressure for one further period of ten minutes.

04. Once the bleeding has stopped, and with the casualty still leaning forwards, clean around their nose with lukewarm water. Advise casualty to rest quietly for a few hours. Tell them to avoid exertion and, in particular, not to blow their nose, because this could disturb any clots.

05. If bleeding stops and then restarts, help the casualty to reapply pressure.

06. If the nosebleed is severe, or if it lasts longer than 20 minutes, arrange to take or send the casualty to hospital.

## Amputation

What is amputation?

This is where a limb has been partially or completely severed. With correct treatment in many cases the limbs may be reattached.

What should I do?

01. Control Blood loss by applying direct pressure.

02. Dress with sterile dressings.

03. Call 999/112.

04. Collect severed part and place in a plastic bag wrapped in a cloth and place in ice, write the casualties name and time of accident on the container, hand to the emergency services.

05. **DO NOT** wash the severed limb.

06. **DO NOT** place directly on ice.

## Crush Injuries

What are crush injuries?

A crush injury may include fractures, internal bleeding and swelling. The force of the crushing may also cause impaired circulation, result in numbness at or below the injured site.

If the casualty is trapped for long lengths of time complications may result. Prolonged crushing may cause extensive tissue damage, more dangerously toxic substances may build up, if released suddenly into the circulation these toxins may cause kidney failure, this is known as the crush syndrome, and can be fatal.

What should I do?

01. If under 15 minutes you can release the casualty.

02. Control any bleeding or fractures.

03. Treat for shock.

04. Call 999/112.

05. If over 15 minutes make the casualty comfortable and wait for professional help unless the casualty is not breathing.

06. Monitor and record vital signs.

## Bruising

What is bruising?

Bruising is where there is bleeding into the skin or bleeding into tissues beneath the skin. Bruising can develop over days or straight away. Be aware that bruising can indicate deeper injuries such as fractures or soft tissue injuries.

What should I do?

01. Place injured part into a comfortable position.

02. Apply a cold compress for 10 minutes.

03. Keep the bruised area raised and supported.

# Managing External & Internal Bleeding

## Abdominal Injuries

Causes of abdominal injuries are:

+ Blunt or penetrating trauma often caused by a severe blow.
+ Evisceration where the abdominal organs protrude out of an open wound.

All cases should be aware of the casualty going into shock. Also be aware of internal bleeding.

### How do I recognise Abdominal Injuries?

### Sign & Symptoms

+ Blunt/Penetrating trauma
+ Mechanism of injury (MOI)
+ Pale cool and clammy skin
+ Signs of shock
+ Rapid weak pulse
+ Rapid & shallow breathing
+ Casualty may guard the abdominal area and may be maintaining abnormal body rigidly.

### Evisceration

+ MOI
+ Pale cool and clammy skin
+ Signs of shock
+ Rapid weak pulse
+ Rapid shallow breathing
+ Anxiety
+ Nausea

### What are my aims?

+ To reduce the reaction
+ To open the airway and promote breathing
+ Monitor the casualty
+ Obtain good history of the incident. Pass onto emergency services.

### What should I do?

01. Call 999/112
02. Control any bleeding
03. Ensure any protruding objects are stabilised
04. Apply suitable dressing
05. If possible lay the casualty down flat with their knees bent. This will ease the pressure off the abdomen
06. If casualty is unresponsive place in recovery position.

### Points to note

These can be little pain associated with these types of wounds and the casualty may be fully mobile.

Casualties suffering blunt or penetrating abdominal injury may also be suffering incontinence

There may be a faecal odour present if in the case of evisceration organs protruding and have been lacerated.

```
Caution
If a penetrating object is present.
DO NOT attempt to remove it. This may be
stemming  the blood loss.
DO NOT apply pressure to it. This may push
the object further into undamaged tissue.
DO NOT apply dressing which will stick to an
eviscerated wound, as this will cause further
damage.
DO NOT attempt to push eviscerated organs
back into the casualty.
```

# 07 Managing Bone Joint & Soft Tissue Injuries

This section describes how fractures occur and the various different types of fracture injury. It examines the difference between fractures and dislocations and describes the first aider's response to these types of injuries. It discusses how to recognise a soft tissue injury and how to provide relevant first aid.

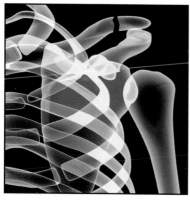

## Content

## Fractures & Dislocations

### What is a fracture and a dislocation?

The bones forming the skeleton provide support, protection, make and store blood cells and minerals, and make movement possible.

Where one bone meets another there is a joint with ligaments and a surrounding area of soft tissue supporting it.

A broken bone is called a fracture. A fracture can occur either by a direct or indirect force on the body. A direct force fractures the bone at the impact site.

An indirect fracture is where the force is transmitted through the body and fractures a bone elsewhere. This is important in first aid, as there may be an injury away from the impact site.

When there is a fracture there is usually accompanying soft tissue damage either to the muscle, tendon, or ligaments.

When a bone is displaced from its natural position in a joint, it is termed a dislocation. Your action for a dislocation is to steady and support the area and **DO NOT** attempt to put back in.

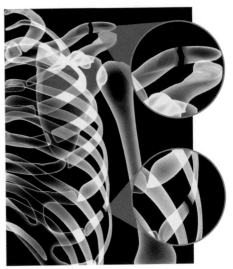

*When there is a fracture there is usually accompanying soft tissue damage either to the muscle, tendon, or ligaments.*

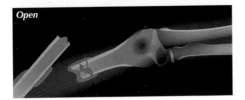

### Types of fracture:

+ **Simple** where there is a clean break and the bones are in alignment.

+ **Closed** where there are multiple bone fragments at the site of the break and the skin is intact.

+ **Open** where there are multiple bone fragments at the site of the break and the fractured bone has broken the skin's surface.

  If the skin is broken there is a risk of external bleeding and more importantly of infection entering the wound.

+ **Complicated** which may involve damage to associated vital organs and major blood vessels as a result of a fracture.

## How do I recognise a fracture or dislocation?

+ History of a fall, a twist or a severe blow
+ Pain and tenderness at the site of the injury
+ A shortening or deformity of the bone
+ Lack of movement in the area (be cautious though as this is not always the case)
+ Signs associated with the fracture site e.g. difficulty in breathing in fractured ribs
+ Nausea
+ Swelling
+ Crepitus (a grating feeling)
+ Signs of hypovolaemic shock

## What should I do?

01. Check for danger, response, airway, breathing and circulation; if there is an open wound protect yourself by using gloves.
02. Support the area and keep it as still as possible.
03. Control any external bleeding but do not apply pressure to any bone protruding through the skin.
04. Lightly cover any open wound with a sterile dressing, packing around any protruding bone.
05. Call emergency medical services if required.
06. Assess for shock as there could be severe blood loss even if it is not apparent and follow hypovolaemic shock guidelines.
07. Stay with and observe the casualty and reassure.
08. Do not give the casualty anything to eat or drink.
09. Check for circulation below the injury e.g. if the skin is pale, capillary refill after finger pressure does not occur within two seconds, or if there is no pulse below the injury, urgent hospital attention is required.
10. Fractures around the nose, mouth or jaw are complicated as blood could compromise the airway.

    Lean the casualty forwards and support the affected area.

    Do not tie anything around the jaw.

## Soft Tissue Injuries

### What are soft tissue injuries?

Soft tissue injuries are those that damage the structural elements of muscles, ligaments, tendons and the vessels supplying these tissues. The amount of bleeding from a torn tissue is dependent upon its blood supply.

Muscles have a rich blood supply and it is more likely that a large bruise will form in the muscle than in an injury to the less vascular tendons and ligaments.

| | |
|---|---|
| **R** | Rest |
| **I** | Ice |
| **C** | Comfort |
| **E** | Elevation |
| **R** | Referral |

### How do I recognise a soft tissue injury?

+ A history of a blow, twist or fall
+ Pain
+ Heat
+ Swelling
+ Redness or obvious bruising
+ Reduced movement

### What should I do?

+ Check for danger, response, airway, breathing and circulation; if there is external bleeding protect yourself by using gloves.

+ **Rest** - Ensure that the area injured is rested as quickly as possible.

This helps to reduce the blood flow to the tissues and helps prevent further damage. *See Fig.1*

*Fig.1*

+ **Ice** - Apply ice to the injured area. This helps to reduce bleeding and helps to reduce muscle spasm and pain.
*See Fig.2*

Ice should not be applied directly to the skin as this can cause a cold burn; a thin wet towel is ideal.

The ice should be applied for 10 minutes and reapplied as required.

Ice should not be applied to open wounds, over the heart area and to people who are sensitive to the cold.

> **Caution**
> Severe sprains and strains can exhibit the same symptoms as a fracture if unsure treat as a fracture.

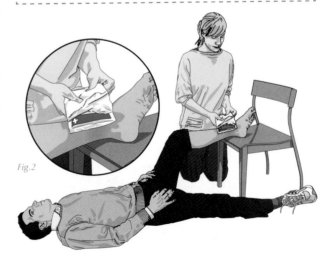

*Fig.2*

*Fig.3*

+ **Comfort/Compression** - If the soft tissue injury is to a limb the area should have a comfort dressing applied to it.

Comfort assists in stopping any further damage to the area.

This needs to be firm but not too tight to restrict circulation.

You can check circulation by observing the temperature, colour, and sensation of the limb below the comfort dressing. *See Fig.3*

+ **Elevation** - This helps to reduce swelling by assisting venous return. *See Fig.4*

+ **Referral** - A first aider should always refer the casualty to his / her doctor, Occupational Health Nurse or hospital for further assessment.

+ Check circulation every 10 minutes.

*Fig.4*

# 08 Burns

This section discusses the different types of burn that can occur in the working environment. It describes the first aid response that is required including the protection of the first aider from chemical burns.

## Content

# Burns

## What happens in a burn?

The skin is the largest human organ. It has two layers, the epidermis the outer protective layer, and the dermis the inner layer. The dermis contains blood vessels, hair follicles and sweat glands.

The function of the skin is to protect the body from infection, assist in temperature control and experience sensations such as pain.

## Causes of burns

+ **Dry** e.g. by a flame, cigarette, or friction
+ **Scald** e.g. by water or hot liquid
+ **Electrical** e.g. by high and low voltage

+ **Cold** e.g. frostbite or liquid nitrogen
+ **Chemical** e.g. fumes or gases
+ **Radiation** e.g. sun, welding or x-ray

Depth of burns can be superficial, partial thickness, or full thickness. It is possible to have several depths in one burn.

## How do I recognise a burn?

+ History of an accident or working with one of the potential causes of the burn, such as electricity.
+ Blood vessels leak and fluid collects under skin (blister), this may break and ooze.
+ If a large area is burnt a lot of fluid (plasma) can be lost and cause hypovolaemic shock
+ The area can swell, this can be dangerous for the airway if there are burns to the face, neck and mouth.
+ There may be pain although not always. Pain may not occur with deep burns.
+ If a burn surrounds an area it can cause constriction which is especially dangerous around a limb or the neck.
+ There is a risk of infection where the skin is broken.

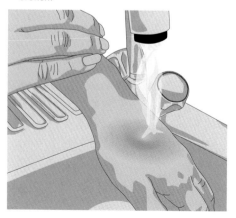

## What should I do?

01. Check for danger (e.g. electricity, fire or chemical) and take appropriate action to protect yourself.
02. Check response, airway, breathing and circulation.
03. Cool with cold water over the area for at least 10 minutes ensuring all the burnt area is flooded. **DO NOT** use ice.
04. Remove any jewellery that may constrict the area as it swells.
05. Ensure the casualty is aware that it has been removed and put in a safe place.
06. Cover the burn with kitchen film or place a clean plastic bag over a foot or hand.
07. Apply the kitchen film lengthways over the burn, not around the limb because the tissues swell.
08. If you do not have these, use a sterile or clean non-fluffy dressing.
09. Reassure the casualty and seek medical advice if appropriate.
10. In a severe burn call the emergency medical services as soon as possible.
11. Do not burst blisters, apply dressings that may stick to the wound, remove clothing that has stuck to the skin, or apply any lotions or creams.

# Burns

## Depth Of Burns

**Superficial**

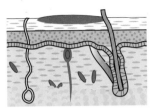

This affects the outer layer of skin. This results in redness and swelling.

These usually heal well with appropriate first aid and medical assistance is not usually required, unless the burn covers a large area or if the first aider is concerned.

**Partial thickness**

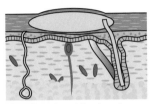

This affects the epidermis and usually results in a raw area with blistering.

Medical treatment is required following first aid.

**Full thickness**

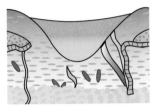

This affects all layers and there is nerve and tissue damage.

Urgent medical attention is required.

## Burns Requiring Hospital Treatment:

+ If the casualty is a child.
+ All full thickness burns.
+ All burns involving the feet, hands , face or genital area.
+ All burns that extend around a limb.
+ All partial thickness burns larger than 1% of the body surface - size of the casualty's palm of hand.
+ All superficial burns larger than 5% of the body surface - 5x the area of casualty's palm of hand.
+ Burns with a mixed pattern of depth.
+ If you are unsure about the extent or severity of the burn.

## Electrical Burn

### What is an Electrical burn?

Burns can occur when electricity passes through the body. Electrical burns can cause surface damage at the point of contact or at the point where the electrical current enters and exits the body. Internal damage can also occur between the point of entry and exit.

Identifying the entry and exit points can assist in identifying possible hidden internal injuries that may have occurred.

### What should I do?

01. Ensure there is no danger from the electricity. Do not approach a casualty injured by high voltage electricity unless you have been informed the electricity has been turned off.

02. Call 999/112.

03. There may be both an entry and exit wound.

04. The heart may have an irregular beat therefore all casualties should seek medical advice.

### Points to note

In the case of high voltages electrocution there is extreme risk to the rescuers. **DO NOTHING** if it puts yourself in danger. Assume the role of crowd control. Keep everyone back at least 18 meters.

## Cold Burn

### What is a Cold burn?

Cold burns can occur when skin comes into contact with an object that is extremely cold. Prolonged contact with cold objects can be sufficient to cause damage to the skin and underlying tissue.

As a result the skin can blister and may cause permeating tissue damage. Frostbite is an example of an extreme case of a cold burn.

### What should I do?

01. Warm the area slowly using body heat.
02. Cover with a sterile dressing.
03. Seek medical advice.

## Chemical Burn

### What is a Chemical burn?

When corrosive chemicals come into contact with the skin they can cause skin irritation, burns or tissue damage if the chemical penetrates the skin.

The most severe instances of chemical burns are likely to occur in industrial environments but chemical burns can also occur in the home.

A number of household products including dishwasher tablets, oven cleaners and paint stripper can cause chemical burns if there is prolonged contact with skin.

### What should I do?

01. Ensure the area is safe and that you are protected from the chemical.
02. This may involve you using personal protective equipment (PPE).
03. All workplaces should have a data sheet or COSHH sheet for the chemicals used and this will state any specific PPE and first aid action required.
04. The area needs to be flooded with water for 20 minutes ensuring that there is no contamination from the chemical to other parts of the body.
05. All chemical burns require hospital treatment.

# 09 Poisoning

This section discusses the different types of poisoning that can occur in the working environment. It shows how to recognise poisoning and how to provide relevant first aid.

## Content

## Poisoning

### What is poisoning?

Poisoning is where a foreign substance enters the body in sufficient quantities to do harm.

Poisons come in many forms such as liquids, gases, and solids.

Poisoning can be accidental such as during a chemical or gas leak, or a substance may have been taken on purpose.

### Poisons enter the body through:

+ **Inhalation** - a chemical in gas form.
+ **Ingested** - a chemical on a worker's hand may transfer to their mouth if they are not careful about their work practices.
+ **Absorption** - a chemical absorbed through the skin/eyes.
+ **Injection** - accidental injection, bee sting or animal bite.

## Common Signs For Poisonous Substances

The signs below indicate substances that can causes chemical burns to the skin. Products or containers displaying any of these symbols should be handled with care and in accordance with manufacturer instructions.

**Dangerous chemicals**

**Harmful chemicals**

**Danger Acid**

CORROSIVE

8

TOXIC GAS

2

OXIDIZING AGENT

5.1

TOXIC

6

POISON

6

# Poisoning

## Recognising Poisoning

### How do I recognise poisoning?

All employees should be aware of which chemicals they are working with and the resultant symptoms should these chemicals enter the body. This information is found in the chemical data sheet.

The signs and symptoms will be dependent upon the substance and how it has entered the body.

### Inhalation

+ Difficulty in breathing.
+ Coughing.
+ Burns around the nose and face.

### Absorption

+ Burns on the skin or chemical spilt on the clothing.

### Ingestion

+ Burns around the lips and mouth.
+ Abdominal pain.
+ Bleeding from the gut seen either by vomiting blood or blood in the stools.

### Injection

+ Puncture mark on the skin.

### General recognition of poisoning

These will be dependent upon the poison.

+ Watering eyes and nose.
+ Swelling of the throat.
+ Difficulty in breathing.
+ Sweating.

+ Irregular heart beat.
+ Altered responsive state.
+ Vomiting and abdominal pain.
+ Seizures.

### What should I do?

01. Beware of danger, this may mean wearing appropriate Personal Protective Equipment (PPE).
02. The casualty may need to be removed from the chemical hazard before starting your first aid checks, e.g. if they have fallen into the chemical or if there is a chemical gas leak.
03. Check the casualty's response, airway, breathing and circulation.
04. If the chemical is on the casualty's face and resuscitation is required a face shield will be needed to protect the first aider from the chemical.

    If a respirator is being used as part of the PPE, the first aider will be unable to administer rescue breathing and a Bag and Mask Resuscitator with a clean supply of air or oxygen will be needed (Additional training to carry out this procedure will be required).
05. Give appropriate first aid dependent upon the symptoms found e.g. treat as an unresponsive casualty.
06. If a specific poison is suspected, take a copy of its data sheet to the hospital with the casualty.

## For inhalation of a poison

01. Ensure the casualty is in a clean supply of air as soon as possible.

## For a poison on the skin

01. Remove contaminated clothing whilst ensuring that you do not contaminate further areas of skin.

02. Assist a responsive casualty to an emergency shower and douse the area with water as for chemical burns.

03. If the casualty is unresponsive the decontamination will need to take place once they have been placed in the recovery position.

04. Where no shower is available improvise with a hose or a water container. Ensure that clean uncontaminated water continually flows over the contaminated area of the body.

05. Douse the contaminated area with water for 20 minutes ensuring the contaminated water does not spill onto a non-contaminated area.

06. At the same time call the Emergency Medical Services (EMS) by dialling 999 / 112. Inform the EMS of the chemical hazard.

## Ingested poison

01. Ask the casualty what they have ingested.

02. **DO NOT** encourage the casualty to vomit.

03. Give sips of water

04. Collect any vomit this could be of use to the hospital.

## For poison in the eye

01. Immediately douse the eye with water from either an eyewash shower, tap or eyewash bottle for 20 minutes.

02. Ensure the water is running over the eye and draining away from the unaffected eye, to prevent contamination.

03. Try to wash under the eyelids. Cover the eye with an eye-pad or first aid dressing and seek medical help.

# 10 Other Injuries

This section looks at other injuries that can occur. It looks at eye injuries, how to recognise them and the action required dependent upon the injury sustained. Head injuries are also discussed and the importance of prompt first aid action if a serious injury is suspected. Finally, neck and spinal injuries are explored.

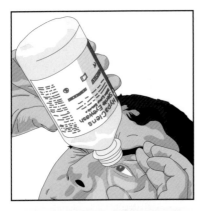

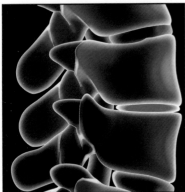

## Content

## Eye Injuries

### What are eye injuries?

Eye injuries occur from dust, metals, chemicals, bruising or lacerations. Caution needs to be taken as what may appear to be a minor injury could have more serious consequences within the eye.

### How do I recognise eye injuries?

+ History of injury or accident.
+ Watering and frequent blinking.
+ A red eye, bruising or bleeding.
+ Distorted vision.

### What should I do?

#### Dust or dirt

01. Gently separate the eyelids and examine every part of the eye for obvious injury.
02. Wash the eye out with cold clean water or eye wash, letting the water run away from the unaffected eye until the grit or dust is removed.
03. Cover the eye with an eye pad. The unaffected eye may also need to be covered to help prevent eye movement.
04. Seek medical advice to ensure there has been no damage to the eye.

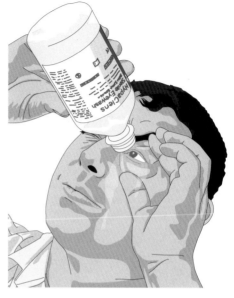

#### Chemical

01. Gently separate the eyelids and examine every part of the eye for obvious injury.
02. Wash out for at least 15-20 minutes or as per the chemical data sheet instructions.
03. Cover the eye with an eye pad. The unaffected eye may also need to be covered to help prevent eye movement.
04. Seek medical advice to ensure there has been no damage to the eye.

#### Foreign body

01. Do not remove any foreign body stuck in the eye or contact lenses.
02. If there is a large foreign body in the eye immobilise the eye by covering around the object and refer the casualty to hospital.
03. Seek medical advice to ensure there has been no damage to the eye.

## Head Injuries

### What is a head injury?

The nervous system consists of the brain and spinal cord and the peripheral nervous system. The brain controls all the body systems and is essential to life. It receives and interprets internal and external messages and governs the body's systems to adapt to these messages.

A blow, impact or shake of the head can cause a head injury. All head injuries are potentially serious even if at first the person may appear to be fully recovered.

## Three Different Kinds Of Head Injuries:

### What types of head injuries are there?

**There are three different kinds of head injuries - Concussion, Cerebral compression and Skull fracture.**

### Concussion

This is where there has been a temporary disturbance in the brain, due to the brain being shaken within the skull. A person does not have to have been unresponsive to have concussion.

Concussion can have potentially serious consequences and should always be treated with caution.

### How do I recognise concussion?

+ History of a blow to the head or a fall
+ Mild Headache
+ Dizziness
+ Nausea
+ Disturbed vision

+ Loss of memory
+ Brief unresponsiveness
+ Confused
+ Repeating the same questions

### What should I do?

01. Check for danger, response, airway, breathing and circulation; if there is external bleeding protect yourself by using gloves.

02. If the casualty is unresponsive treat as previously discussed.

03. Check for the signs and symptoms of concussion and if any are noted seek medical advice.

04. Be aware that someone with a head injury can appear well but can deteriorate very quickly. Therefore, refer the casualty to appropriate medical advice especially if they have any of the above signs or symptoms.

05. Any clear, straw coloured fluid from the ear or nose can indicate a fractured skull and urgent removal to hospital is necessary.

## Cerebral compression

This is when the brain becomes compressed due to either the brain swelling or through bleeding around the brain, or the skull compressing the brain as in a compressed skull fracture.

This can be following a head injury or during an illness such as a stroke. It can occur immediately or slowly over several hours or days. The casualty can deteriorate quickly and it is often fatal.

### How do I recognise cerebral compression?

+ A history which may indicate a head injury, infection or tumour intense headache
+ Severe dizziness and headache
+ Lack of co-ordination
+ Nausea and vomiting
+ Could lead to unresponsiveness
+ Unequal pupil reaction to light stimuli
+ Unable to track a moving finger with the eyes.
+ Noisy breathing

### What should I do?

01. Check for danger, response, airway, breathing and circulation; if there is external bleeding protect yourself by using gloves.
02. If the casualty is unresponsive treat as previously discussed.
03. Check for the signs and symptoms of compression and if any are noted seek medical advice.
04. Be aware that someone with a head injury can appear well but can deteriorate very quickly. Therefore, refer the casualty to appropriate medical advice especially if they have any of the above signs or symptoms.

## Skull fracture

### How do I recognise a skull fracture?

+ History of a blow to the head
+ Skull deformity, possible open wound
+ Headache
+ Uneven pupils
+ Evidence of clear discharge from the ears or nose (CSF - Cerebral Spinal Fluid)
+ Altered levels of response

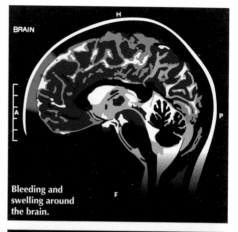

Bleeding and swelling around the brain.

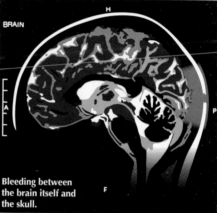

Bleeding between the brain itself and the skull.

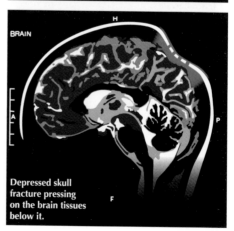

Depressed skull fracture pressing on the brain tissues below it.

# Other Injuries

## What should I do?

01. Call EMS 999/112
02. Maintain airway treatment
03. Keep the head as stable as possible, do not remove headgear unless there is an urgent need to do so, for example; when access to the mouth is required for rescue breathing when breathing has stopped.
04. Move the casualty using a log rolling technique where there is an urgent need to do so for example; the casualty is unable to maintain their own airway.
05. The casualty's ability to maintain their airway breathing and circulation always takes precedence over the risk of making the spinal injury worse.
06. Observe and record the casualty's airway, breathing and circulation.

## Spinal Injuries

### What are spinal injuries?

The spine is made up of vertebrae; they allow movement within the spine and protect the spinal cord. The spinal cord is part of the nervous system which passes messages to and from the brain.

If the spinal cord is severed this causes paralysis below the site of the injury. Temporary damage can be caused if the spinal cord is pinched or if a disc has prolapsed and is pressing it.

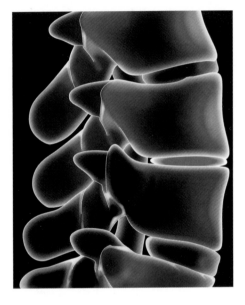

### How do I recognise a spinal injury?

+ History of a fall, accident or trauma to the back or neck
+ Pain in the back or neck
+ Restricted movement of the neck or back
+ Abnormal curve of the spine
+ Tenderness on touching the spinal area

### How do I recognise a severe spinal injury?

+ Loss of control and feeling in the limbs
+ Loss of sensation or tingling in the limbs / pins or needles
+ Breathing difficulties
+ Incontinence
+ Beware, in some severe spinal injuries the casualty may initially be able to move

## What do I do?

01. Check for danger, response, airway, breathing and circulation; if there is an open wound protect yourself by using gloves. Then:

### For minor neck and back pain

01. Assist the casualty to a comfortable position. This is usually lying down to help ease the pain.
02. Advise the casualty to seek medical aid.
03. Call emergency medical services if required.
04. Do not move the casualty if you suspect a spinal injury.

### For spinal injuries

01. Do not move the casualty if you suspect a spinal injury; keep them as still as possible.
02. Call the emergency medical services as soon as possible.
03. Keep the head as stable as possible, do not remove headgear unless there is an urgent need to do so, for example; when access to the mouth is required for rescue breathing when breathing has stopped.
04. Move the casualty using a log rolling technique where there is an urgent need to do so for example; the casualty is unable to maintain their own airway.
05. The casualty's ability to maintain their airway breathing and circulation always takes precedence over the risk of making the spinal injury worse.
06. Observe and record the casualty's airway, breathing and circulation.

# 11 Conditions

This section looks at common diseases that occur in the work place. Starting with cardiac conditions, it describes how to recognise and give first aid in these situations. It continues to discuss common diseases such as asthma. Factors in the environment such as temperature are looked at and how these may affect a casualty.

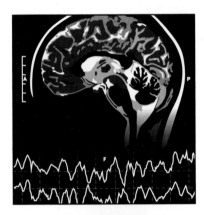

## Content

## Cardiac Conditions

What are cardiac conditions?

**There are two different kinds of conditions - Angina and Heart Attack.**

### Angina

This is usually a chronic condition. It occurs when there is not enough oxygenated blood getting to the heart muscle. Exercise, anxiety, stress or the cold can bring it on.

### How do I recognise angina?

+ Weakness

+ Shortness of breath

+ A pain across the chest which usually eases with rest

+ Vice like chest pain which may spread to one or both arms, the jaw and the top of shoulders

### What should I do?

01. Sit the casualty down well supported with their knees up (w position) or comfortable position.

02. Ask them if they have tablets or spray, which they use for the pain and let them use it.

03. Obtain medical aid urgently.

04. Ask bystander to fetch an AED.

05. Reassure the casualty and don't fuss.

06. Monitor and record airway, breathing and circulation, be prepared to carry out CPR if necessary.

07. Place in the recovery position if they become unresponsive.

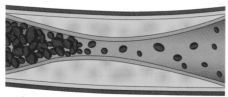

**Angina** - *Vessels can become narrowed restricting the flow of oxygenated blood to the vessels in the heart.*

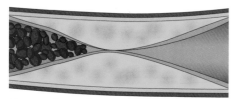

**Heart Attack** - *Vessels can become completely blocked, stopping the flow of oxygen.*

### Heart attack

A heart attack occurs when a clot suddenly closes off the supply of blood to part of the heart muscle.

### How do I recognise a heart attack?

+ Chest pain is often sudden, crushing, "vice like" which does not ease with rest

+ Breathlessness

+ May have pain in the left arm or jaw

+ Nausea

+ Look of fear

+ May complain of indigestion

### What should I do?

01. Obtain medical aid urgently stating to ambulance control that it is chest pain.

02. Sit the casualty down well supported with their knees up or a comfortable position.

03. Give casualty a 300mg aspirin, advise to chew slowly. Do not give aspirin if allergic to it.

04. Ask bystander to fetch an AED.

05. Reassure the casualty, don't fuss.

06. Constantly monitor airway, breathing and circulation. Be prepared to carry out CPR if necessary.

07. Place in the recovery position if they become unresponsive.

## Diabetes

### What is diabetes?

Diabetes is a medical condition that affects the body's ability to produce insulin. An essential hormone that controls how glucose (blood sugar) is distributed to cells and tissues in the body.

There are two main types of Diabetic emergency that you may come across in the workplace - **Hyperglycaemia** and **Hypoglycaemia**.

### Hyperglycaemia

Results from high blood sugar or not enough insulin. Onset occurs gradually.

### How do I recognise hyperglycaemia?

High blood sugar is typically caused by a failure to administer sufficient insulin. Especially common after meals, it can be identified by the following symptoms:

+ Drowsy and dehydrated

+ Complaints of feeling nauseous and vomiting

+ Rapid breathing

+ An urge to urinate

+ Extreme thirst, usually accompanied by a distinct 'acetone' odour on the breath

+ Dry and warm skin

**The onset of a hyperglycaemic emergency occurs very gradually.**

+ It is rare that a casualty will become completely unresponsive as such extreme deterioration may take a number of days.

### What should I do?

### In an unresponsive casualty:

01. Call an ambulance.

02. Check the casualty's Airway, Breathing and Circulation (ABC).

03. If necessary, place the casualty in the recovery position or perform CPR.

### In a responsive casualty:

01. Call an ambulance.

02. Reassure the casualty.

03. Try and keep the casualty alert.

04. If in doubt and responsive, give sugar.

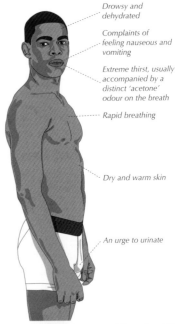

*Drowsy and dehydrated*

*Complaints of feeling nauseous and vomiting*

*Extreme thirst, usually accompanied by a distinct 'acetone' odour on the breath*

*Rapid breathing*

*Dry and warm skin*

*An urge to urinate*

| HYPERGLYCAEMIA | High Blood Sugar Level or not enough insulin | Excessive blood sugar levels are due to too much sugar or carbohydrate in the diet, too little insulin, or infections |
|---|---|---|

## Hypoglycaemia

Results from low blood sugar or too much insulin. Onset occurs very rapidly.

## How do I recognise hypoglycaemia?

Low blood sugar is typically caused by over-administration of Insulin medication or missing a meal / other irregular eating patterns. It can also be caused by exercise and stress and is identified by the following symptoms:

+ Display of confused / aggressive behaviour
+ Deteriorating levels of response / responsiveness
+ Complaints of feeling faint
+ Strong pulse with a rapid rate
+ Sweaty /clammy feeling to the surface of the skin, sometimes pale
+ Complaints of feeling hungry

**The onset of a hypoglycaemic emergency occurs rapidly.**

+ If urgent action is not taken the casualty will become completely unresponsive and may even suffer from a seizure.

## What should I do?

The priority is to raise the casualty's blood sugar levels, in the form of a sugary drink or snack.

## In an unresponsive casualty:

01. Call an ambulance at the earliest opportunity.
02. Check the casualty's Airway, Breathing and Circulation (ABC).
03. If necessary, place the casualty in the recovery position or perform CPR.
04. DO NOT attempt to raise an unresponsive casualty's blood sugar levels by administering food or drink.

    This may block the airway.

## In a responsive casualty:

01. Ensure the casualty is seated.
02. Encourage them to drink a sugary drink or eat sugary foods. This will raise blood sugar levels.
03. As the casualty begins to respond to sugar intake and show signs of recovery, continue to encourage them to eat and drink.
04. Seek medical advice.

*Useful recourse: www.diabetes.org.uk*

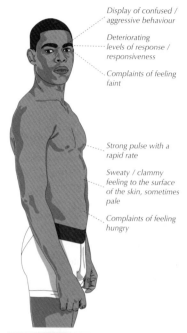

Display of confused / aggressive behaviour

Deteriorating levels of response / responsiveness

Complaints of feeling faint

Strong pulse with a rapid rate

Sweaty / clammy feeling to the surface of the skin, sometimes pale

Complaints of feeling hungry

| HYPOGLYCAEMIA | Low Blood Sugar Level or too much insulin | Low blood sugar levels caused by too little sugar and carbohydrate in the diet in relation to the body's requirement, or too much insulin. |
| --- | --- | --- |

## Seizures

### What are seizures?

Seizures occur when the normal electrical activity in the brain is interrupted. This interruption can occur for a variety of reasons. Epilepsy is the most common cause of seizures.

Other causes include:

+ Reduced supply of oxygen to the brain
+ Reduced supply of glucose to the brain
+ Drugs and alcohol
+ Diseases that affect the brain
+ Head injuries

Seizures do not always result in the casualty dropping to the floor and convulsing. The effects of seizures can, in fact, be quite mild and result in little more than a reduction in the casualty's levels of response and general awareness.

There are two types of seizures - **Minor Seizures** and **Major Seizures**.

### Minor Seizures

### How do I recognise minor seizures?

Casualties may display the following symptoms:

+ Reduced levels of awareness and response
+ Eyes remain open but unable to focus
+ Mild twitching movements in the limbs, head and facial features
+ Grinding the jaw
+ Absence moment
+ Blank stares
+ Unaware of surroundings

### What should I do?

01. Get the casualty to sit down on the floor. This will help to prevent injury if the seizure should worsen and the casualty collapses.

02. Most casualties will show full signs of recovery within a few minutes of the seizure.

03. If the casualty does not show any signs of recovery after 10 minutes, call for an ambulance.

04. It is rare that a major seizure follows a minor seizure. If this does occur, however, follow the advice outlined.

## Major Seizures

### How do I recognise major seizures?

The onset of a major seizure can usually be identified by a tensing of the casualty's body followed by a sharp fall to the floor. Once on the floor the casualty's back may begin to arch and the following symptoms displayed:

As the casualty begins to recover they will feel confused and disoriented while their levels of awareness and response improve. It is also normal for the casualty to feel sleepy and exhausted.

### What should I do?

01. The casualty may have an aura, where they experience a warning, this could be anything from a strange feeling to an unusual smell or taste.

02. The casualty will almost definitely collapse during a major seizure. Try to control the fall.

03. Ensure the safety of the casualty by removing any objects that may cause injury if they are struck.

04. Place padding under the head of the casualty. Improvise if necessary by using clothing.

05. DO NOT place anything in the casualty's mouth.

06. Loosen any clothing that may restrict the airway.

07. Time the seizure. Seizures will normally last up to 3 minutes but can last longer.

**When the seizure has subsided:**

01. Check the casualty's Airway, Breathing and Circulation (ABC).

02. If unresponsive and breathing normally or semi-responsive, place the casualty in the recovery position (see opposite). Perform CPR if not breathing.

03. Can also put a blanket over casualty to preserve modesty.

04. Reassure the casualty whilst continuing to monitor the ABC and any other injuries.

**Call for an ambulance if:**

+ Any concerns with ABC's.

+ You feel unable to cope with the situation.

+ The casualty is not known as an Epilepsy sufferer and you suspect the seizure may be caused by something else such as a head injury.

+ Convulsions last for 5 minutes or more.

+ The casualty suffers from a number of smaller seizures.

+ No signs of recovery after 10 minutes.

+ The casualty injures himself/herself.

+ You are unsure they are an epileptic.

*For more information: www.epilepsy.org.uk*

## Stroke

### What is a stroke?

A stroke occurs when the blood supply to the brain is impaired by a blood clot, an embolism or haemorrhage. It is a medical emergency.

Casualties may display the following symptoms:

+ A sudden, severe headache
+ Flushed face
+ Slurred speech
+ Drooping of the mouth
+ Possible incontinence
+ Weakness or paralysis to one side of the body
+ Unequal pupils

Fig.1

### What should I do?

01. Check for danger, response, airway, breathing and circulation.

02. Assess **FAST** test

 **F** ⟩ Face

 **A** ⟩ Arms

**S** ⟩ Speech

**T** ⟩ Telephone

+ **F** = Face - Ask casualty to smile, has their mouth or eye dropped? *See fig.1*

+ **A** = Arms - Hold both arms up, let go and ask casualty to hold arms up, there may be a drop or drift of an arm. *See fig.2*

+ **S** = Speech - Ask casualty some questions, you may get slurred speech.

+ **T** = Telephone - Call 999 / 112, tell them you're carried out the FAST test. A casualty may fail any one part of this test, to suspect a stroke.

03. Place in a comfortable position and reassure the casualty that help is on its way.

04. Monitor the whole time until help arrives.

Fig.2

## Transient Ischaemic Attack

### What is a Transient Ischaemic Attack (TIA)?

Know as a minor stroke and has roughly the same symptoms .The only difference is the effects may only last from a few minutes up to 24 hours and will appear to make a full recovery.

If in doubt treat as a stroke as they should seek medical assessment.

## Heat Exhaustion

### What is heat exhaustion?

Heat exhaustion occurs when there is a loss of water and salt through excessive sweating.

This may occur when someone has been in a hot environment or exercising.

### How do I recognise it?

+ Sweating
+ Pale and clammy skin
+ Nausea
+ Cramps in the limbs
+ Dizziness, weakness

### What should I do?

01. Move the casualty to a cooler environment.
02. Lay them down and raise their legs.
03. Remove excess clothing.
04. Give a cool drink.
05. Monitor and record vital signs.
06. Seek medical help if vital signs worsen call 999/112 for emergency help.

## Heat Stroke

### What is heat stroke?

This is a serious condition where sweating will stop as the body becomes too hot. This can lead to unresponsiveness and can be fatal.

### How do I recognise it?

+ Flushed, hot dry skin
+ Restlessness, confusion
+ A full, bounding pulse

### What should I do?

01. Move the casualty to a cooler environment.
02. Remove excess clothing.
03. Call 999/112 for emergency help.
04. Wrap the casualty in a wet sheet.
05. Fan and/or sponge the casualty.
06. Monitor and record vital signs.
07. If the casualty becomes unresponsive place them in the recovery position.

## Hypothermia

### What is hypothermia?

The body retains heat by shivering, raising the fine hairs on the skin, constricting blood vessels and burning fat.

In the workplace this may occur from environmental factors especially where the worker is exposed to cold and / or wet conditions.

Cold injuries can range from mild frostbite to severe hypothermia where the body temperature has dropped below 35°C. If the core body temperature falls below 26°C this is nearly always fatal.

### How do I recognise hypothermia?

+ Shivering, however in severe hypothermia the shivering stops
+ Pale and cold skin
+ Disorientation
+ Slow shallow breathing
+ Weak pulse
+ Heart may stop

### What should I do?

01. Check for danger, response, airway, breathing and circulation.

02. Remove wet clothing and replace with dry clothing or blankets where possible.

03. Call 999/112 for emergency help.

04. In frostbite, warm the body part under your arm or next to your skin. The fingers and toes can be extremely painful so be cautious.

05. In hypothermia, shelter the casualty from the elements.

06. Use a foil blanket to assist in warming.

07. Give warm drinks or high energy foods such as chocolate if available.

08. Use your own body heat if necessary.

09. DO NOT warm the casualty too quickly as this causes the blood vessels to dilate and can cause shock.

## Fainting

### What is fainting?

Fainting is a brief loss of responsiveness which is caused by a temporary reduction of blood supply to the brain.

This happens when the heart slows down and blood vessels dilate. Unlike Shock, recovery from a faint is usually rapid and complete.

### Causes of Fainting

+ Emotional distress
+ Lack of food
+ Long periods of inactivity
+ Fatigue
+ Pain or fright
+ Warm atmospheres

### How do I recognise fainting?

+ A brief loss of responsiveness
+ Collapse to the floor
+ A slow pulse
+ Pale, cold, sweaty skin
+ Prior to collapse casualty may complain of nausea, feel weak, dizzy and light headed

### What should I do?

01. Lay the casualty down and raise and support legs, returning blood to the brain.
02. Maintain airway, breathing and circulation.
03. Allow plenty of fresh air, open windows if necessary.
04. If casualty recovers, reassure and help to sit up and recover gradually.
05. If the casualty does not recover quickly or you are unsure, place into the recovery position and dial 999 / 112 for an ambulance.

# 12 Sports First Aid

This section covers the important pre-event checks for sports activities which can help to minimise the risk of injury, together with the steps to take should the worst happen.

## Content

## Roles & Responsibilities

As a first aider you are taking on a role of responsibility. The fear of your actions being questioned or challenged should not arise providing you:

+ Keep your skills and knowledge up to date.

+ Act within the training you have been given.

+ Act in a professional manner.

There is currently no legal framework covering sports first aid, although you are encouraged to undertake training with a qualified instructor. It is also prudent to contact any sports governing bodies for local rules or arrangements that would be specific to your sporting activity.

### Why do we need first aiders in sport?

The main reason being that accidents, illnesses and injuries can occur at anytime and the sporting environment is no exception.

In fact with the growth of the number of people involved in leisure pursuits, it is inevitable that at times there will be injuries.

## Pre-event Precautions

Here are some considerations which may be of use when planning a sporting event, to help you provide first aid cover more effectively.

**Make sure it is clear who is responsible for providing adequate first aid provisions. They must ensure that the following considerations are made:**

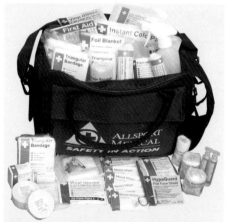

+ Is the first aid kit or touchline bag fully stocked? (Each bag should be tailored for the sports activity being undertaken, but some key provisions should always include a number key items (see First Aid Touchline Bag content).

+ Is there a stretcher available?

+ Is ice and water available?

+ Is there a first aid room? If yes, is it adequate for the sports activities taking place?

+ How would an ambulance access the site if required?

+ Where is the nearest hospital?

+ Is this information available to the visiting team?

+ Is there a doctor or other first aider present during the game?

+ Where is the nearest telephone if a mobile phone does not work?

### First Aid Touchline Bag

Each bag should be tailored for the sports activity being undertaken, but some key provisions includes

+ Pocket mask

+ Disposable gloves

+ Squirty bottle with water

+ Scissors & safety pins

+ Gauze swabs

+ Triangular bandage

+ Glucose tablets

+ Drinks

+ Clinical waste bag

# Sports First Aid

## Recording Incidents

Incidents must always be recorded in your accident book and a copy should be given to the organisers and hospital/ambulance crew.

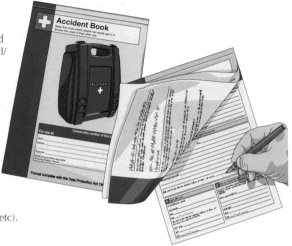

Details should include:

+ Full name and address of player.
+ Date of birth.
+ Date and time of incident.
+ Report of injury (what happened)?
+ Witnesses.
+ Details of injury sustained.
+ Treatment given.
+ Disposal of player (hospital, home etc).
+ Name and signature of first aider.

## Checking Players

+ Are they injury free?
+ Have they been ill prior to the event?
+ Do they have a medical condition?
+ Have they removed jewellery?
+ Do they wear any protective equipment that may be difficult to remove in the event of an accident?
+ Are they chewing gum?
+ Are they physically / mentally prepared i.e. not dehydrated?

## Playing Environment

+ Is the playing surface safe and suitable?
+ Is it free from any debris or anything else that may cause injury?
+ What are the climatic conditions?
+ Is the equipment to be used in good order?
+ Is correct footwear being worn?

## Identifying & Managing Injuries

### Sports Injuries

The injuries mostly associated with sport are as follows:

+ Fractures and dislocations.
+ Soft tissue injuries.
+ Facial and head injuries.
+ Spinal injuries.
+ Cuts and wounds.

Treat all injuries as you have been trained to do and in accordance with information provided in the rest of this manual.

### Spinal Injuries

Spinal injuries should be suspected when a casualty is involved in one of the following mechanisms of injury and the history of the accident indicates that it may be present.

+ Fall from a height (e.g. Diving board, fall from horse, pole vault) .
+ Fall from a fast moving vehicle (motorcycle).
+ Compression force injuries i.e. diving into the shallow end of a swimming pool.
+ Force rotation of spine (twisting action).
+ Hyper flexion or extension (i.e. collapsed rugby scrum).
+ Other severe injuries e.g. head injuries and loss of responsiveness.
+ Severe damage to equipment i.e. cars, motorcycles, bikes, crash helmets etc due to acceleration or deceleration forces.

### Assessment of Neurological Injuries

+ Pain over site of injury.
+ Deformity of site of injury.
+ Weakness, numbness, tingling sensation in limbs.
+ Possible paralysis of limbs or partial loss of movement.
+ Loss of sensation below the point of injury.
+ Body fixated in position.
+ Incontinence.
+ Breathing problems.
+ Muscle spasms.

## Treatment of Injuries

### What should I do?

01. Check for danger.
02. Check for response (While holding head to stop neck rotation).
03. Shout for help (summon assistance).
04. Check for airway.
05. Establish breathing.
06. If casualty is breathing immobilise spine and head. Do not move casualty unless clearing the airway requires it.
07. If casualty is responsive check for neurological disability.
08. Check for other injuries.
09. Monitor condition.
10. Keep casualty warm and as comfortable as possible.
11. Reassure casualty until arrival of the ambulance.

## Continued Participation

### When Should a Player Cease from Continuing to Participate?

As a general rule we can follow these guidelines to see whether a player should continue or not:

+ If there is any loss of function.
+ If there is a loss of strength.
+ If the player continues to complain of pain.
+ If the wound continues to bleed.
+ If the player begins to suffer from either extremes of body temperature.
+ If the player suffered any loss of or a reduced level of responsiveness.
+ If the player has suffered a head injury and shows any signs or symptoms of such.

### Other Points to Consider

+ If it is a team sport the player may feel pressurised into staying on and not letting the team down.
+ Peer pressure from other team members.
+ What position do they play in? i.e. a finger injury to an outfield player may allow him to continue to play football but if the same injury occurred to the goal keeper this may not be possible.

**Remember if a player continues in the sport despite advice always hold an end of session check.**